iROBOT

CLIVE GIFFORD

CARLTON KIDS

HOW TO USE THIS BOOK

Discover an amazing world with Augmented Reality

This book, together with the free app, uses the very latest Augmented Reality (AR) technology to mix the real and virtual worlds together. Viewed through your mobile device, the robots will appear to come to life as interactive animations.

Wow! What do I need?

To run the Augmented Reality animations, all you need is this book, the app and a mobile device that meets the minimum requirement specification below.

It's easy! Here's what you need to do...

1 Download the free iRobotAR app from www.apple.com/itunes or www.android.com. apps to your mobile device. Open the app and go to the home page.

2 Tap the iRobotAR button to activate the AR and discover 4 fantastic AR experiences.

3 There are 4 robot AR Activation Pages in this book. Hold your mobile device over each of the Activation Pages to release incredible Augmented Reality robots!

This product will work with the following devices:

- The following Apple devices running iOS 6.0 or above: iPhone 4S or above; iPad2 or above; iPod Touch 5th Gen. or above.
- Android devices with both forward- and backward-facing cameras using Android 4.0 and above, and ARMv7 processors.
- INTEL based devices are not supported.
- Battle mode will require an active wi-fi connection.

BUILD A BOT

CREATE YOUR OWN CUSTOMIZED ROBOT AND TAKE IT FOR A WALK.

Step 1 – Select from a range of heads, legs, arms, colours and extra features to build your own bot.

Step 2 – Take it for a walk using the controls on your screen, or tell it to perform a series of actions by arranging the code buttons in order.

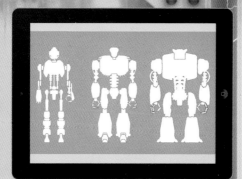

FLY A DRONE

DIRECT A SEARCH-AND-RESCUE DRONE AROUND YOUR HOME.

Step 1 – Once your drone has appeared, switch it on and press the buttons to make it take off and land. Use the joystick to control its flight.

Step 2 – Fly your drone around to locate the targets.

MEET A HUMANOID ROBOT

RELEASE A WALKING, HUMAN-SHAPED ROBOT.

Step 1 – Tap the start button and your robot will appear. Use the onscreen joystick to make your robot move around.

Step 2 – With this amazing life-size mode you can take a few steps back and then tap the zoom button to make your robot grow to full size! The life-size robot can't walk but you can walk around it and explore the robot from different positions. Get a friend to stand next to it and take a photograph.

BATTLE WITH BOTS

GRAB A FRIEND WITH A SECOND DEVICE, EACH PICK YOUR ROBOT AND LET THE BATTLE BEGIN!

Step 1 – Open the app on both your devices. The first user should select their robot and activate it in the battle arena. Then the second user should select their robot, and select the first user's device from the list of friends shown.

Step 2 – You'll see two robots on screen but only be able to control yours, using the joystick. You can either attack or defend in the battle. The loser is the first robot to run out of energy.

NEED SOME HELP? Check out our useful website for helpful tips and problem-solving advice:
www.carltonbooks.co.uk/icarltonar/help

A WHOLE LOT OF BOTS

> Working onboard the International Space Station, the free-flying SPHERE robots are rounded 25cm-wide (9.8in) cubes that move by firing jet thrusters powered by carbon dioxide gas.

Robots are adaptable machines that can be programmed to perform really useful work for humans. Many robots perform tasks people find difficult, unpleasant or deadly. There are more than 10 million robots on the planet, and that number is increasing all the time.

POWER AND MOVEMENT

Robots can be entirely mobile or they might have some moving parts, such as a robot arm that is bolted to a factory floor but has jointed parts that it can move. A robot's moving parts are mostly powered by electric motors or power systems using compressed liquids (hydraulic) or compressed air (pneumatic). Each direction that a robot part can move in is known as a degree of freedom (DOF). Many robot arms have joints that give the robot five or six degrees of freedom.

> Rather than needing large computer programs to be rewritten each time their job changes, some robots can be taught new tasks by a teaching pendant wielded by a human worker.

> Sony's QRIO robot's many joints are powered by 38 small motors. The robot can walk, trot and pick itself up if it falls.

ROBOT BRAINS

A robot has sensors that gather information, much like your senses do. This data is sent to the robot's controller — usually a computer or microprocessor, running programs created by robotics researchers. The controller organizes all the parts of the robot, makes decisions and instructs the parts to move or work in certain ways to complete the robot's job. It lets the robot react to events around it so it can keep working.

ROBOT EXPLORERS

Robots can venture to places that are difficult or dangerous for humans to reach. They have been sent into raging infernos, deep into space, to explore other planets, and, in the case of Dante and NASA's VolcanoBot 1, into the mouths of volcanoes. Some, like Kaiko and Nereus, have explored the ocean depths, more than 10km (6.2 miles) below sea level. Others, such as Pyramid Rover, have crept through narrow stone tunnels in ancient Egyptian pyramids that are thousands of years old.

> RoboHOW's PR2 robot can flip pancakes using a spatula gripped in its hand. The robot learned this task by comparing instructions on the Internet with its own database of commands.

> Dante II climbed into the mouth of the Mount Spurr volcano in 1994 to collect gas samples without putting human scientists at risk.

GRIPPING STUFF

Many robots have parts that interact with their environment, such as a gripping hand on the end of a robot arm. These are called end effectors. They could be a scraper or drill enabling a space robot to obtain a small sample of a distant planet. Surgical robots can be fitted with various medical tools.

UNDER CONTROL

Most robots aren't completely autonomous. This means that although they have some control and perform parts of their tasks themselves, they need some human supervision or control to guide them. Some robots, such as many flying drones, bomb disposal robots and underwater ROVs (remote operated vehicles) are fully remote-controlled by a person.

DID YOU KNOW?

'Robot' comes from the Czech word 'robota', meaning forced labour. Many robots do dull jobs with perfect accuracy, and faster than humans can. An example is Robot-Rx – this selects the correct medicines to prepare prescriptions of drugs for patients. It can prepare over 2,500 different prescriptions in a working day.

> Robotic drones can fly forward, backward or hover, carrying scientific instruments or cameras to record information.

ROBOTS AT WORK AND PLAY

Robots are great at performing dull, precise or dangerous work, again and again. Almost two million robots work in industries, and some interact with humans in fun ways, such as playing sports or music and solving puzzles.

> Around 80 per cent of all the work needed to produce a car can be performed by robots.

CAR STARS

The very first working robot was called Unimate. It handled hot metal parts in a car factory in 1961. Thousands more have followed in its footsteps. Robots now perform many jobs in car factories, such as putting together car bodies – making over 4,000 welds on each one – and spraypainting vehicles.

ARMIES OF ARMS

Robot arms are the most common type of robot in factories. They can be fitted with different tools, from rivet guns to grippers, which can pick up and pack objects. The Fanuc M-2000iA/1 robot arm can lift up to 1,199kg (2,643lb) – that's more than the mass of some cars.

> The ABB IRB 340 FlexPicker whizzes over a conveyor belt, picking and examining food products. It can pick up 400 individual objects per minute.

> Baxter can be re-programmed via the computer in its chest. Its two arms can perform a wide range of jobs — from assembling fiddly electronic products to heavy lifting.

OUT AND ABOUT

Not all working robots are found in factories. Some are found on farms, in the form of robotic milking machines and flying mini crop-sprayers. Others work in mines and construction, or travel down unpleasant sewers and chemical pipelines, checking for leaks and other issues.

PLAY TIME

Some robots play games or perform tasks we think are fun. They are designed to learn how to play chess, football or solve fun puzzles to test their controllers, sensors and software. This helps scientists build smarter and more effective working robots.

FLEXIBLE WORKMATES

Unlike humans, industrial robots can work 24 hours a day. They don't go on strike or need lunch or toilet breaks – just the occasional maintenance overhaul. Some, like the Baxter robot, are extremely versatile and designed to operate alongside human workers.

> A Rubik's Cube puzzle can take people hours to solve. In 2014, the Cubestormer 3 robot solved the puzzle in just 3.25 seconds!

HEAVY METAL

Some robots can even play musical instruments. Several robot bands have been formed, including Compressorhead from Germany and Z-Machines from Japan. This latter group includes a six-armed drummer called Ashura, and Mach, a robot that plays the guitar using its 78 fingers, which are powered by compressed air. Rock on!

> The third member of Z-Machines is Cosmo, a keyboardist that triggers notes using lasers.

SUPER SENSORS

Just as humans receive information from their eyes, ears and other sense organs, robots require sensors to function. These devices gather information and pass it back to the robot's controller for it to make decisions.

❯ Two robots compete for the ball during a football game. Such games provide stern tests for robots, which have to scan the pitch and map an ever-changing environment as the ball and other robots move.

WHERE AM I?

Some robots have simple vision systems that let them follow lines on a floor, for example to follow a route around a factory. Other robots can recognize their surroundings or objects they are working on, using high resolution cameras. These more complex vision systems send digital data back to a robot's controller.

Some robots can build up a map of their environment, measuring their distance from objects or places using ultrasound or infra-red sensors. In addition, many mobile robots have satellite navigation receivers built in so they can work out where they are.

❯ Hitachi's EMIEW 2 mobile robot can travel at 6km/h (3.7mi/h) as its cameras and sensors alert it to any obstacles in the 80cm-tall (32in) robot's path, from walls to moving people.

SELF-AWARE

Your brain, senses and nervous system give you extraordinary powers of awareness. Your brain knows where every part of you is at any one time. To do something similar, robots need to have a combination of sensors giving them different pieces of information.

Joint encoders, for example, can detect the angle of a robot arm's wrist or elbow. Tilt sensors can detect by how much a robot is leaning, while accelerometer sensors can measure the speed of movement in a certain direction. By putting together these sorts of sensors, robots can, for example, be given a sense of balance.

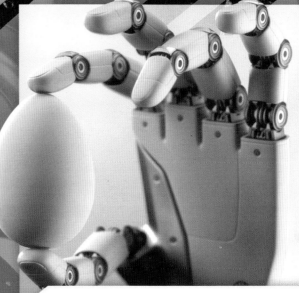

BUMP AND TOUCH

A robot that navigates itself, for example a household vacuum cleaner, has simple sensors that react and send signals when it bumps into an obstacle in its way. But robots that perform delicate medical work or handle fragile objects need much more complex sensors. These can measure the amount of force a robot uses to touch or grip an object.

> Robot hands have tiny servos or electric motors to move each finger joint precisely, so that a robot can use the right amount of grip and force to hold delicate objects, such as a fresh egg.

SPEEDY SENSORS

Some robots need all their sensors to work together quickly. Researchers test the speeds of their systems by building robots that can play ball sports. Robots that can track balls and wield bats to play table tennis have been developed, while Toshiba has built a volleyball-playing robot. The Dynamic Brain robot can also juggle. Robots even have their own football World Cup – RoboCup – which included over 500 teams in 2015.

> A Topio 3 humanoid robot from Vietnam plays table tennis. Its high-speed cameras and sensors track the fast-moving ball to provide the robot with the data it needs to move its bat to hit the ball as it arrives.

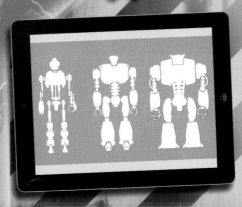

AUGMENTED REALITY

Build your very own robot! Customize its features and then see it on the move.

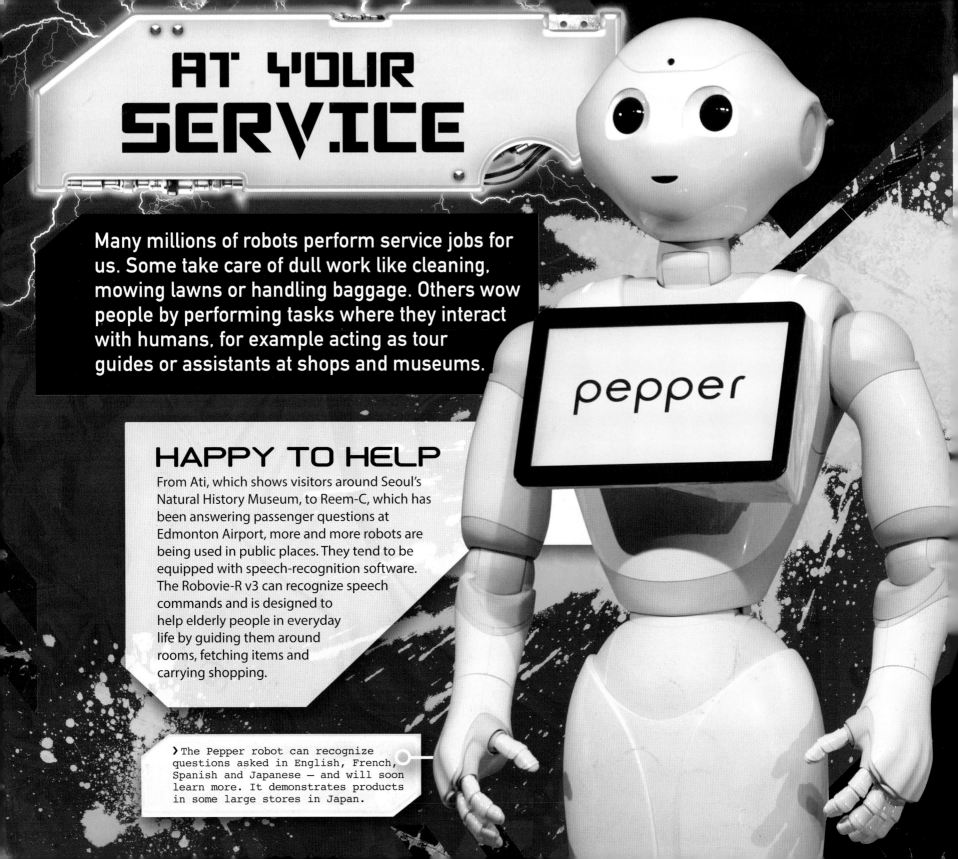

AT YOUR SERVICE

Many millions of robots perform service jobs for us. Some take care of dull work like cleaning, mowing lawns or handling baggage. Others wow people by performing tasks where they interact with humans, for example acting as tour guides or assistants at shops and museums.

HAPPY TO HELP

From Ati, which shows visitors around Seoul's Natural History Museum, to Reem-C, which has been answering passenger questions at Edmonton Airport, more and more robots are being used in public places. They tend to be equipped with speech-recognition software. The Robovie-R v3 can recognize speech commands and is designed to help elderly people in everyday life by guiding them around rooms, fetching items and carrying shopping.

> ❯ The Pepper robot can recognize questions asked in English, French, Spanish and Japanese — and will soon learn more. It demonstrates products in some large stores in Japan.

> The newest robot from the makers of the A.L.O. robot butler is called the Relay. It works with staff to deliver and carry items from one person to another.

BUTLERS AND VALETS

The Yobot is a 6m-long (19.7ft) robot arm that works as a left-luggage attendant in a New York hotel. It scans bags and places them in lockers while guests leave the hotel. The A.L.O. is a robot butler that can carry room service and other items to a guest's room, equipped with a map of the hotel stored in its memory and the ability to use the hotel's lifts. The 90cm-tall (2ft 11in) robot automatically phones a guest's room to say it is arriving and accepts tweets on Twitter instead of tips!

CAR PARK VALET

Ray the Robot works at Düsseldorf Airport, where it parks cars in tight spaces, allowing the car park to house more vehicles. Ray picks up each car using its two sets of fork-lift forks and puts it into a spare space. It retrieves cars so they are ready and waiting for returning passengers.

> Ray scans each vehicle using lasers to know its precise size. The robot can squeeze in up to 60 per cent more cars in the car park than if human owners parked them.

CLEAN MACHINES

Robots clean our houses and our swimming pools. But they can also clean on a larger scale. A pair of Sabre robots sandblasts the framework of the Sydney Harbour Bridge in Australia to clean away rust and old paint – a job that would be unpleasant and potentially dangerous for humans.

> The two Sabre robots on the Sydney Harbour Bridge build 3D maps of the areas they are working on, then blast away old paint and rust.

> A number of robots in the Robot Restaurant work in the kitchen, cooking noodles and deep-frying dumplings.

ROBO RESTAURANT

The Robot Restaurant, in the Chinese city of Harbin, employs 20 robots. Some act as waiters, following routes marked out in white lines on the restaurant floor to deliver trays of food. Another entertains diners by singing songs.

DID YOU KNOW?

Carl is a humanoid robot – made of spare industrial robot parts – able to select different ingredients as it mixes and makes cocktails in a bar in Ilmenau, Germany.

ALMOST HUMAN

Ask someone to think of a robot and, chances are, most will picture a humanoid robot – a metal person. As some robots are built to look and act more like humans, other projects are giving humans robot-like abilities.

BALANCING BOTS

Walking is an activity most humans take for granted, but it is not so easy for robots. Being a bipedal (two-legged) machine means that a humanoid has to balance on one leg as it lifts and moves the other – easy for us, but hard for a machine.

Breakthroughs, however, have led to humanoids able to walk, climb stairs and, in the case of HOAP-2 and NAO, even perform martial-arts moves. Honda's Asimo remains the Usain Bolt of humanoids. In 2014, it broke its own record for the fastest-running two-legged robot, reaching 9km/h (5.6mi/h).

> NASA's Valkyrie robot is 1.9m (6ft 3in) tall and has a mass of 120kg (265lb). It is designed to climb ladders, use tools and walk over uneven ground. Future humanoid robots are expected to work alongside astronauts in space.

AUGMENTED REALITY

Meet a humanoid robot and see how it moves. Watch it grow to life size and then take a photo!

LEARNING LIKE US

Some humanoid robots study how humans learn and how robots might build up knowledge in similar ways to us. Robota is an American robot, shaped like a baby, which watches human actions and learns to imitate them.

Another learning robot, iCub, can feel, grasp and identify objects and learn words connected to those objects. More than 20 iCubs are currently at work in robotics labs in Europe, trying to advance ways robots can learn for themselves.

> The iCub robot is about 1m (39in) tall and contains 53 motors that move its body parts. It has already passed tough tests, such as navigating through 3D mazes.

WEARABLE ROBOTS

Your skeleton strengthens your body from the inside, but robotic exoskeletons are worn on the outside to give people extra strength or stamina – the ability to work for long periods without tiring. Some, such as Ekso Bionic's eLegs, help people who've lost strength or movement in their bodies. Other exoskeletons, such as Panasonic's Powerloader or the HULC, are being developed to give soldiers or industrial workers extra strength to lift heavy objects – as much as 100kg (220lb) – with ease.

> The HULC exoskeleton has powered legs made of titanium, which helps its wearers carry heavy loads but is flexible so that wearers can still squat, crawl, and lift things with their upper bodies.

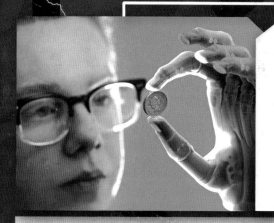

> The i-limb hand can automatically switch to one of 24 different types of grip, from pinching a small item gently between thumb and forefinger to firmly gripping a tennis racquet. It can hold and manipulate items up to 90kg (198lb).

BIONIC PEOPLE

The latest advanced prosthetics (artificial body parts) borrow from robotics to create more lifelike and versatile artificial arms, hands and legs. Touch Bionics' i-limb ultra prosthetic hand, for example, is packed with microprocessors and sensors, can move each of its fingers independently and adjust the strength and type of grip speedily, just like a human hand. It can be controlled by the wearer's muscles or a smartphone app.

ROBO SPIES

Watch out, there are robot spies about. These gather sensitive information without risking human agents' lives. The robots can be fitted with cameras, night vision, listening devices and sensors to detect nuclear radiation, weapon launches, or chemical weapons.

THE WAY AHEAD
The military uses land robots, such as the Talon and Asendro, to travel ahead of human forces and check for ambushes or booby traps. In addition, small, rugged robots can be thrown over high walls, land and right themselves. Throwbot XT and Recon Scout XL are two examples. They scuttle around on spiked wheels, sending back information.

> Asendro can climb stairs and move through buildings, seeking out intruders or vital information using its high-resolution cameras.

> UAVs can either be controlled remotely by a pilot on the ground, or fly autonomously.

SPIES THAT FLY
Thousands of aerial robots, known as UAVs (Unmanned Aerial Vehicles), are already hard at work. Many, such as Global Hawk and the MQ-9 Reaper, can fly on long missions over enemy territory. They use cameras to spot troop movements, new weapons and other secrets. Smaller UAVs, such as drones that hover like helicopters, are used by many law-enforcement agencies to track suspects and search from the air.

SEA SPIES

A growing number of underwater robots are being used in seas and lakes to spy. AUVs (Autonomous Underwater Vehicles) can stay submerged for weeks at a time. Other underwater spy bots, which are under development, will one day blend in with the marine environment. Cyro, for example, looks like a giant jellyfish, and GhostSwimmer is disguised as a tuna fish.

> GhostSwimmer is 1.5m (4.9ft) long, has a 45kg (99lb) mass and operates at depths up to 91m (300ft).

STAY SECURE

Some robots operate as security guards, stopping spies and intruders. One of the first was Robart III, which had a gun that could fire tranquilizer darts. Today they are usually kitted out with cameras, microphones and thermal imagers, which detect heat given off by machines and living things. Some can communicate with a building's electronics to, for example, close all doors if an intruder is detected.

> With powerful cameras, the K5 can track human intruders and recognize vehicle licence plates. It can send information over wireless networks.

> As well as spying, in the future Robobees may also be used to help pollinate crops.

MICRO SPY

Already, flying robots small enough to fit in your hand are being tested in labs. These include Harvard's Robobees, which are the size of a coin and flap their tiny wings 120 times a second. In the future, some of these tiny spies might record secret meetings through windows or photograph documents using microscopic cameras.

ROBOTS TO THE RESCUE

Robots are great for performing crucial tasks at disaster and emergency sites. They can get to places that humans struggle to reach, and deal with risks such as fire, as well as hazardous materials that would harm human rescuers, such as toxic chemicals.

> Snakebots can wriggle through ducts and pipes in damaged buildings. This type of robot can be fitted with sensors to detect heat given off by living things and so locate survivors.

SEEK AND FIND

When an earthquake, flood or explosion strikes, it can often leave victims trapped underneath debris. Search robots are designed to seek out these victims. Small tracked robots like Packbot can travel over rubble to locate survivors and even carry oxygen or water to them. Snakebots are built of hinged segments, and the PoseiDrone robot has soft, flexible tentacles. Both systems allow robots to squeeze through tiny gaps.

GRIPPING AND RIPPING

The giant Tmsuk T-52 Enryu stands 3.45m (11ft 4in) tall and is designed to clear debris and rescue people. Each of the robot's 6m-long (19ft 8in) arms has eight joints and can lift weights up to 500kg (1,100lb). Powered by hydraulics, they have enough strength to rip a car door off its hinges. This robot's successor, the T-53, cleared rubble in areas of high radioactivity in Japan in 2011, after disaster struck at the Fukushima nuclear power station.

> The Tmsuk T-52 can either be operated by remote control, or by someone from inside the robot itself.

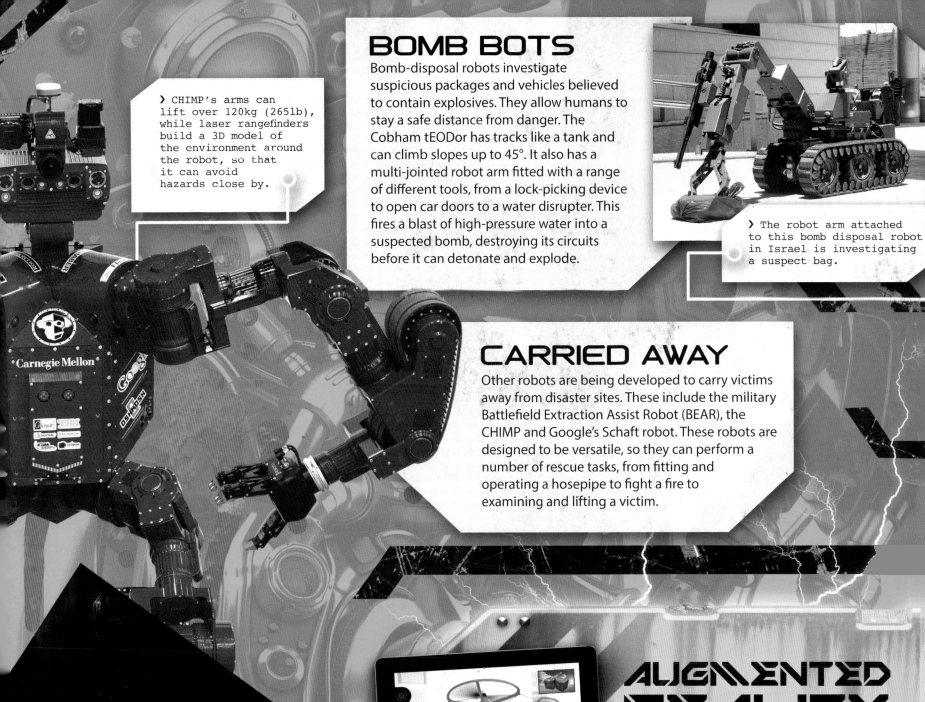

> CHIMP's arms can lift over 120kg (265lb), while laser rangefinders build a 3D model of the environment around the robot, so that it can avoid hazards close by.

BOMB BOTS

Bomb-disposal robots investigate suspicious packages and vehicles believed to contain explosives. They allow humans to stay a safe distance from danger. The Cobham tEODor has tracks like a tank and can climb slopes up to 45°. It also has a multi-jointed robot arm fitted with a range of different tools, from a lock-picking device to open car doors to a water disrupter. This fires a blast of high-pressure water into a suspected bomb, destroying its circuits before it can detonate and explode.

> The robot arm attached to this bomb disposal robot in Israel is investigating a suspect bag.

CARRIED AWAY

Other robots are being developed to carry victims away from disaster sites. These include the military Battlefield Extraction Assist Robot (BEAR), the CHIMP and Google's Schaft robot. These robots are designed to be versatile, so they can perform a number of rescue tasks, from fitting and operating a hosepipe to fight a fire to examining and lifting a victim.

DID YOU KNOW?

A future project, called Ryptide, may use flying robot drones to carry and drop a buoyancy aid to people struggling in water. The drone would be able to reach the person quicker than human lifeguards.

AUGMENTED REALITY

Fly your own search and rescue drone. Navigate the flying robot to locate the targets.

ROBOTS IN SPACE

Sending humans into space is costly and complex – they need food, oxygen and life-support systems. Sending robots is simpler, because they are normally sent on one-way missions, needing no more than an onboard power source to keep them going.

ROVING ROBOTS

Robots that land and explore the surface of a moon or planet are known as rovers. These have to deal with uneven, often rocky ground and have no human help nearby should they break down or roll over. Radio signals to and from Mars, for example, can take minutes, and this delay makes remote-controlling a rover in real time impossible. As a result, Mars rovers have to be largely autonomous. They are sent a target or task from Earth, but the rover controls how it is managed.

> ❯ Curiosity weighs 899kg (1,982lb) and moves across Mars on six wheels with a diameter of 50cm (20in). It uses four pairs of cameras to avoid rocks in its path and carries a science lab to analyze rock and soil samples.

SPACE PROBES

Space probes are machines launched into space to explore the Solar System. Some fly past planets, moons or asteroids, and others orbit around their targets so that their scientific instruments can take photographs, and measure temperatures and other details. This data is sent back to Earth via radio waves, which travel through the huge distances of space at the speed of light.

In 2014, after a ten-year journey across space, the European Space Agency's Rosetta space probe reached Comet 67P/C-G. It went into orbit around the comet but dropped another robotic probe, called Philae, on to the comet's surface.

> ❯ Voyager 1 is the farthest human-made object from Earth, over 19 billion km (12 billion miles) away. Radio signals over that distance take more than 17 hours to reach Earth.

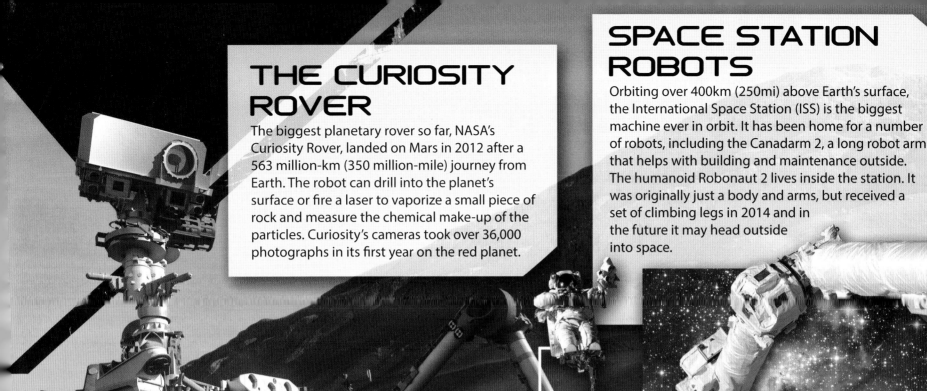

THE CURIOSITY ROVER

The biggest planetary rover so far, NASA's Curiosity Rover, landed on Mars in 2012 after a 563 million-km (350 million-mile) journey from Earth. The robot can drill into the planet's surface or fire a laser to vaporize a small piece of rock and measure the chemical make-up of the particles. Curiosity's cameras took over 36,000 photographs in its first year on the red planet.

SPACE STATION ROBOTS

Orbiting over 400km (250mi) above Earth's surface, the International Space Station (ISS) is the biggest machine ever in orbit. It has been home for a number of robots, including the Canadarm 2, a long robot arm that helps with building and maintenance outside. The humanoid Robonaut 2 lives inside the station. It was originally just a body and arms, but received a set of climbing legs in 2014 and in the future it may head outside into space.

> Astronaut Stephen K. Robinson takes a wild ride on the 17.6m-long (58ft) Canadarm 2, fitted to the ISS. The arm is capable of manoeuvring up to 116,000kg (255,736lb).

FUTURE SPACEBOTS

NASA and other organizations are working on dozens of different robot designs that, one day, may be launched into space. They include giant inflatable robot balls that could be carried around Mars' surface by winds, and folding robots flown flat-packed to the Moon or Mars, which assemble themselves on arrival, then begin work. Spidernaut is an eight-legged bot that might one day clamber over space stations and bases, performing vital maintenance work, while RASSOR is a robot miner designed to dig deep into the Moon's surface.

DID YOU KNOW?

Robotic probes can send back huge amounts of data. In 2011, the LRO space probe sent back 192 terabytes of photos and other information as it orbited the Moon. That would be enough to fill 41,000 DVDs!

SOCIAL ROBOTS

To be truly sociable, robots need to react and interact with humans, have meaningful conversations and understand facial expressions and body language. Such tasks require highly advanced robotics, electronics and software.

SPEAK AND TELL

Robots recognize human speech using software that analyzes sounds gathered by microphones. Robots are good at responding to simple phrases and commands, but at the moment, struggle to understand the meaning of complex sentences. MIT's Jibo, though, can understand many short conversations, read out a person's emails, remind them about an appointment or tell them a story.

> Jibo can recognize people in a home and, over time, store their likes and dislikes in its memory to build up a simple picture of each person's interests.

RECOGNIZING FACES

Robots don't recognize people they have met before unless they are specifically programmed to do so. Robots such as Nexi, NAO and the SociBot-Mini run facial-recognition software. This compares images taken by the robot's cameras with ones stored in its memory to find a match. SociBot-Mini can track up to 12 different people that it recognizes as they move around a crowded room.

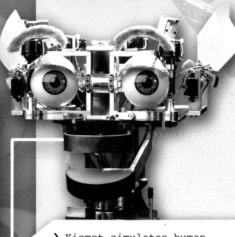

> Kismet simulates human emotions with motor-powered facial features that can register surprise, happiness, sadness, anger and other emotions.

> Kodomoroid is a humanoid robot that reads news and weather reports in a museum in Tokyo, Japan. She is modelled on a real person and covered in silicone that is designed to look like human skin.

EXPRESS YOURSELF

The human face has more than 40 muscles it uses to create many different expressions. Being able to understand others' expressions and create their own is a goal of many social robots. MIT's Kismet robot in the 1990s, Leonardo and the K-Bot in the 2000s and the FACE robot in the 2010s are all expressive robots. Electric motors power features on their faces so that they can show expressions.

HI-TECH TEACHERS

As robots become better at interacting with people, so the number of jobs they can do will increase. Robot tutors may be able to help children with reading. Robot actors wouldn't tire of repeating the same words or forget their lines, while robo-reporters could interview people and relay the interview back to the newsroom. Already, the Japanese robots Kodomoroid and Otonaroid have been demonstrated reading the news.

ROBO CARERS

Many social robots are being developed to provide companions for elderly people. Some, like the furry, seal-like robot Paro, offer the comforts of a pet without having to be looked after. Other, more complex, robots, like Pepper, the Carebot P37 S65 and Kompai, may become active helpers, able to fetch and carry, remind elderly people to take medicines and alert medics if the person is ill. Carebot P37 S65 can even crack jokes to cheer people up.

> RoboThespian is powered by pneumatic motors and can perform songs and speeches or present lectures in museums and other public places.

DR ROBOTS

Robots help save lives every day – from assisting people recovering from illness to performing operations. Other medical robots work behind the scenes, performing repetitive but essential jobs, such as preparing prescriptions or carrying meals around hospitals.

> Twendy-One's strong arms end in four-fingered hands covered in soft material. They can grip fragile objects without damaging them.

NURSEBOTS

Some robots care directly for patients. These nursebots, such as RIBA II, which looks like a friendly bear, can remind patients when to take medicine and help them with their exercises. Twendy-One, a nursebot in Japan, can deliver meals, lift patients out of bed or help patients.

> RIBA II can lift patients weighing up to 80kg (176lb) in and out of bed.

UNDER THE KNIFE

Some robot arms can move much more accurately than a human hand. They can be programmed to cut, probe and grip during operations. This can make surgery more accurate, and sometimes lead to shorter recovery times. Robodoc, one robot surgeon, has helped perform tens of thousands of knee- and hip- replacement operations.

DID YOU KNOW?

In 2010, a 70-year-old man became the first person to have a heart operation performed by the Amigo robot without a human surgeon in the same room. The operation normally takes take eight hours, but the robot completed it successfully in just an hour.

NANOROBOTS

A nanometre is one thousand millionth of a metre. A sheet of paper can be 100,000 nanometres thick. Amazingly, robotic devices called nanorobots or nanobots, measuring just a few nanometres in diameter, may one day be produced. These bots could give an incredible view from inside the human body, detecting diseases in close-up and accurately diagnosing problems with organs such as the heart.

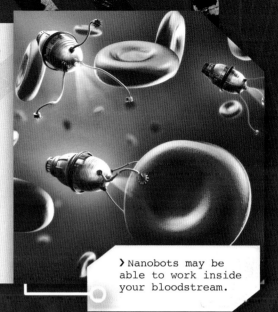

> Nanobots may be able to work inside your bloodstream.

THROUGH THE KEYHOLE

Some robot surgeons perform keyhole surgery – operating through tiny openings in a patient into which they insert cameras and surgical tools. Several thousand Da Vinci robots have performed over 1.5 million operations. They are guided by human surgeons wearing goggles that give them a three-dimensional, magnified view of the operation area.

> The instruments on a Da Vinci robot can bend and rotate far more than the human wrist.

TINY SURGEONS

Future nanobots may be made so small that thousands, even millions, could fit in a syringe and be injected into your bloodstream to begin an amazing journey inside your body. These nanobots could work on individual body cells, zapping diseased tissue, fighting cancers and repairing damaged cells all without surgery. Plaque-busting nanobots may even be able to clean your blood vessels, improving your blood flow and health.

DID YOU KNOW?

In 2014, the University of Texas built a nanomotor small enough to fit inside a single human cell. Such technology may power future nanobots around your body.

ROBO-BEASTS

Living things are very good at what they do, so it makes sense for engineers to copy nature to make robots better. Biomimetic robots are robots modelled on the shape, structure or abilities of living things.

❭ The LS3 robot has sensors that let it follow a leader automatically.

ROACH BOT

Robots that have to scramble over uneven ground are often modelled on spiders or insects, whose many legs make them very stable. Some robots copy the springy, scuttling movement of the cockroach – one of nature's hardiest creatures, which can travel over rough ground easily.

❭ Built mainly of cardboard and with a mass of just 30g (1oz), Velociroach can move swiftly, more than 25 times its body length every second.

ROBOT RUNNERS

Some four-legged animals are good at moving across rough ground and others are fast runners. BigDog and LS3, robots that are built like mules or large dogs, can walk up steep slopes, trot at speed and carry hundreds of kilograms of soldiers' kit. The Cheetah robot, in contrast, is built for speed and has a flexible spine, just like the big cat, which helps transmit more energy to the ground.

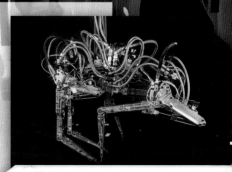

❭ Cheetah holds the world speed record for land robots with legs – 46.4km/h (28.8mi/h) – that's faster than Usain Bolt.

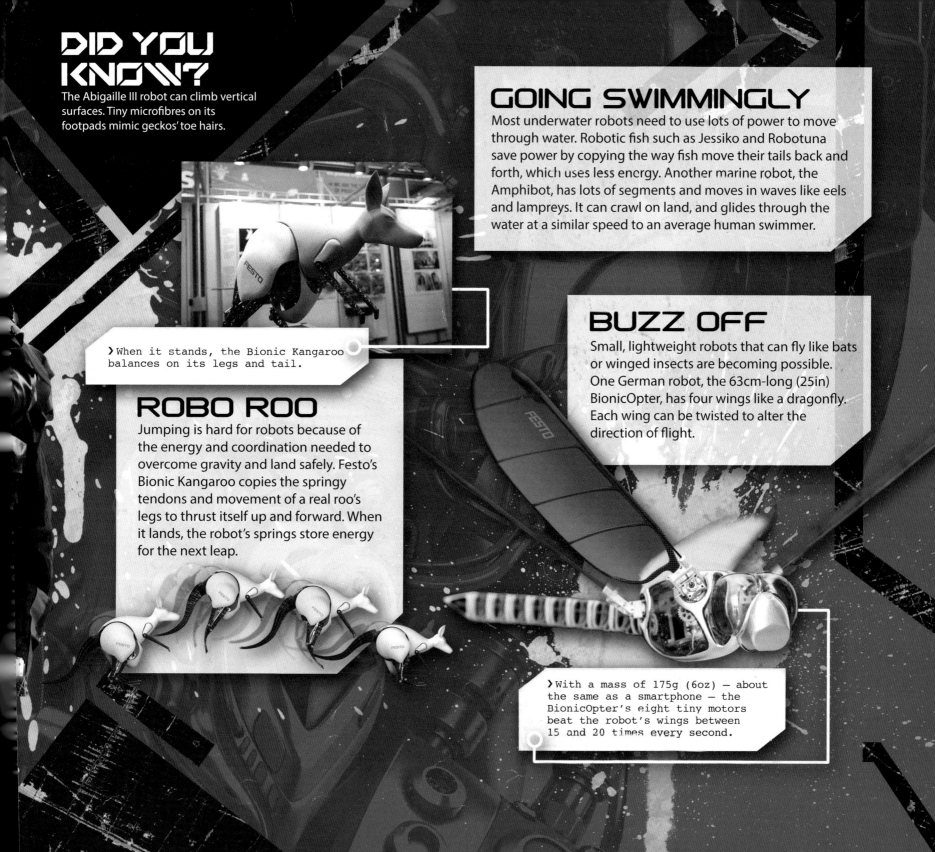

DID YOU KNOW?

The Abigaille III robot can climb vertical surfaces. Tiny microfibres on its footpads mimic geckos' toe hairs.

GOING SWIMMINGLY

Most underwater robots need to use lots of power to move through water. Robotic fish such as Jessiko and Robotuna save power by copying the way fish move their tails back and forth, which uses less energy. Another marine robot, the Amphibot, has lots of segments and moves in waves like eels and lampreys. It can crawl on land, and glides through the water at a similar speed to an average human swimmer.

> When it stands, the Bionic Kangaroo balances on its legs and tail.

ROBO ROO

Jumping is hard for robots because of the energy and coordination needed to overcome gravity and land safely. Festo's Bionic Kangaroo copies the springy tendons and movement of a real roo's legs to thrust itself up and forward. When it lands, the robot's springs store energy for the next leap.

BUZZ OFF

Small, lightweight robots that can fly like bats or winged insects are becoming possible. One German robot, the 63cm-long (25in) BionicOpter, has four wings like a dragonfly. Each wing can be twisted to alter the direction of flight.

> With a mass of 175g (6oz) — about the same as a smartphone — the BionicOpter's eight tiny motors beat the robot's wings between 15 and 20 times every second.

BATTLIN' BOTS

Science-fiction comics and movies often show robot armies in action. While these are fantasy, robots are already in service in many military forces, locating landmines, acting as guards and mapping out hostile territory.

DRONE ZONE

Many UAVs, such as the Predator and Hunter, have already been fitted with air-to-ground missiles. Future robotic planes may be powered by jet engines and be larger, such as the BAE Tarantis, the Dassault nEUROn and the 20,000kg (44,000lb) Northrop Grumman's X-47B.

> In 2014, the Northrop Grumman's X-47B was the first flying robot to make a successful autonomous landing on an aircraft-carrier ship.

> The Japanese Kuratas was designed and built by an artist, but future combat robots might be similar. It fires 6,000 bullets per minute, and can discharge water rockets and fireworks.

IN SERVICE SOON?

Much secrecy surrounds the development of new military robots, but Big Dog, BEAR, LS3 and other strong robot carriers, running on tracks or legs, may soon ferry supplies and weapons into war zones. Some may also recover injured personnel who are in the line of fire – a task planned for Israel's AirMule robot flying ambulance, which is under development.

SENTRY BOTS

Robot sentries are already in service. In 2014, the Samsung SGR-1 robot sentry was installed in the zone of land separating two countries, North Korea and South Korea. Equipped with heat-seeking and movement sensors, it can detect potential intruders from over 2.5km (1.5mi) away. Robot snipers may soon follow. Robots can aim weapons with deadly accuracy.

> The Samsung SGR-1 can be fitted with a machine gun, but this can only be used if a human gives the go ahead.

FUTURISTIC BATTLEFIELDS

In the future, humans may leave the battlefield, and sit instead in distant command centres, observing and controlling robotic forces. These could be swarms of robot scouts on air, sea and land, with large, armoured robot tanks and planes, all programmed to strike together. In urban conflicts, shape-shifting mobile robots might lie low or be able to squeeze through the smallest spaces, before expanding to full size and height to become battle ready.

ROBO-SOLDIERS

Humanoid robots aren't currently practical for outdoor action, but in the distant future, they might serve as soldiers, under human command. The weapons they wield might be aimed at enemy robots rather than people, so could include lasers or devices that disrupt the electronic circuits of their robotic foes. Robo-soldiers might carry small, autonomous UAVs on their bodies, which could be launched and fly unaided to a target, carrying a small bomb or warhead.

AUGMENTED REALITY

Battle with bots! Invite a friend to join you, pick your robots and see who wins.

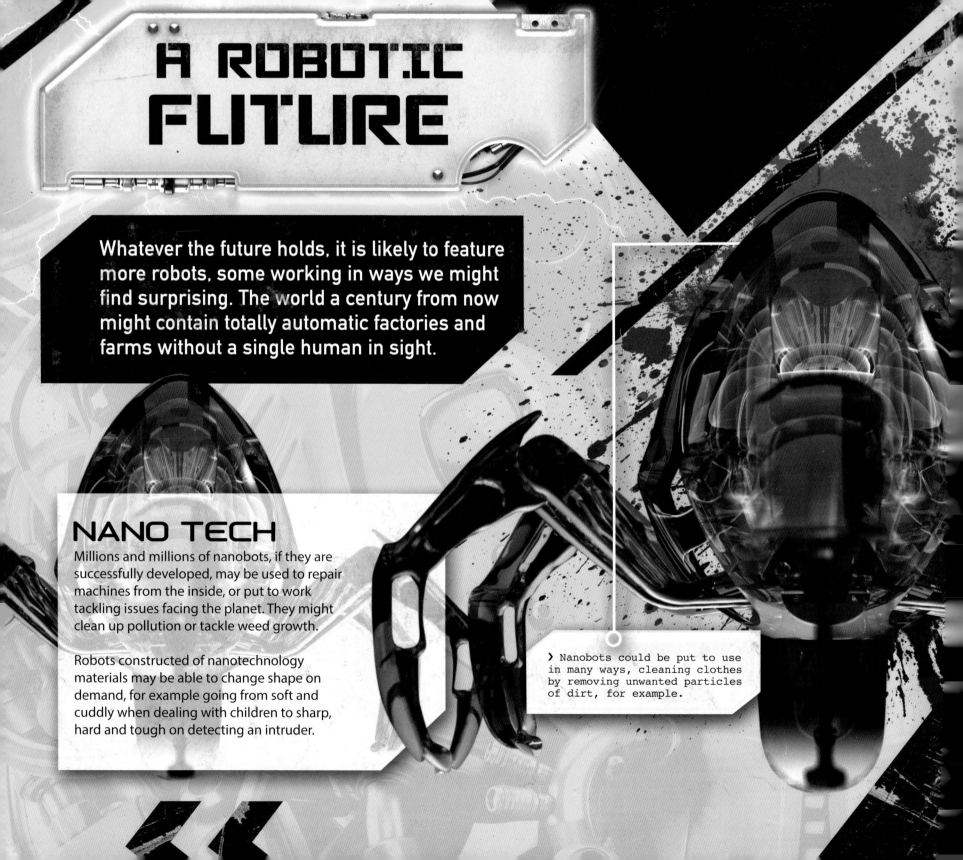

A ROBOTIC FUTURE

Whatever the future holds, it is likely to feature more robots, some working in ways we might find surprising. The world a century from now might contain totally automatic factories and farms without a single human in sight.

NANO TECH

Millions and millions of nanobots, if they are successfully developed, may be used to repair machines from the inside, or put to work tackling issues facing the planet. They might clean up pollution or tackle weed growth.

Robots constructed of nanotechnology materials may be able to change shape on demand, for example going from soft and cuddly when dealing with children to sharp, hard and tough on detecting an intruder.

> Nanobots could be put to use in many ways, cleaning clothes by removing unwanted particles of dirt, for example.